P.K. SUBBAN

MAKING HIS MARK ON THE HOCKEY WORLD

TERESA M. WALKER

First Edition
First Printing, 2019

Book design by Jake Slavik
Cover design by Jake Slavik
Photographs ©: Danny Murphy/Icon Sportswire/AP Images, cover (foreground), 53, 73; Mark Humphrey/AP Images, cover (background), 59, 63, 69; Keith Srakocic/AP Images, 4; John Crouch/Icon Sportswire/AP Images, 7; Eric Canha/Cal Sport Media/AP Images, 9; George Pimentel/WireImage/Getty Images, 12; Lester Balajadia/Shutterstock Images, 17; JC Pinheiro/Icon Sportswire, 20; Ryan Remiorz/Canadian Press/AP Images, 25; Matt Slocum/AP Images, 29; Paul Chiasson/The Canadian Press/AP Images, 30, 92; Anthony Nesmith/Cal Sport Media/AP Images, 35, 80; Nick Loverde/Cal Sport Media/AP Images, 36; Mark Zaleski/AP Images, 40, 55, 66; Graham Hughes/The Canadian Press/AP Images, 42, 46, 48, 50; Alex Gallardo/AP Images, 60; Steve Roberts/Cal Sport Media/AP Images, 75; Cliff Welch/Icon Sportswire, 76; John Russell/National Hockey League/Getty Images, 83, 89; BravoKiloVideo/Shutterstock Images, 86; John Locher/AP Images, 94; James Atoa/Everett Collection/Newscom, 97; Paul Spinelli/AP Images, 100

Design Elements ©: Shutterstock

Press Box Books, an imprint of Press Room Editions.

Library of Congress Control Number: 2018952198

ISBN:
978-1-63494-050-4 (paperback)
978-1-63494-062-7 (epub)
978-1-63494-074-0 (hosted ebook)

Distributed by North Star Editions, Inc.
2297 Waters Drive
Mendota Heights, MN 55120
www.northstareditions.com
Printed in the United States of America

TABLE OF CONTENTS

P.K. Subban patrols the ice during Game 2 of the
2017 Stanley Cup Final.

CHAPTER 1
ONE OF A KIND

He's too showy. Too confident. He falls to the ice too quickly, trying to draw a penalty. He talks too much. Celebrates too much.

He's a hockey villain.

P.K. Subban has heard all the criticisms. He's the player that fans will boo all night long when he's competing against their team. But he's also the guy fans love when he's playing in his home arena.

This theme was on full display in June 2017 when Subban and the Nashville Predators faced the Pittsburgh Penguins. Subban was playing in the Stanley Cup Final—hockey's biggest stage—for the first time in his career.

The Penguins won the first two games to take a 2–0 lead in the best-of-seven series. But in Game 3, the Predators struck back. Subban smothered Penguins star Sidney Crosby, keeping him without a shot.

Nashville routed Pittsburgh 5–1 in that game, cutting the Penguins' lead to 2–1.

Before the players left the ice, Subban skated near Crosby and yelled at him. Crosby yelled back. When reporters asked about what they said to each other, Subban joked that Crosby complained about his breath. Subban drew laughs when he told the story.

"When guys chirp after a game or during a game, it's usually about your game or something personal," Subban said. "But he went on to tell me that my breath smelled bad. I really don't understand why, because I used Listerine before the game. I thought my breath smelled great. At the end of the day, we're going to take the win and move on."

Reporters crowded around Crosby in the Penguins' locker room, eager to hear his take on Subban's comments. However, Crosby kept his answer short.

"He likes the attention, and things like that," Crosby said. "If he wants to make stuff up, what can I do?"

Part of Subban's approach was simple: he wanted to get Crosby thinking about him, and not his own game.

"Every time he's on the ice, I'm going to be in his face. And he's not going to like it," Subban said.

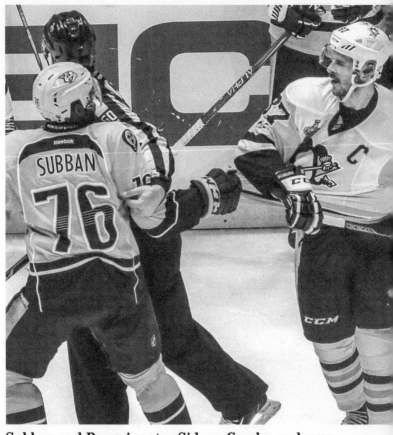

Subban and Penguins star Sidney Crosby exchange a few words after Game 3 of the 2017 Stanley Cup Final.

Even so, Crosby claimed not to notice Subban.

"I haven't seen P.K. much. We haven't been in their zone probably enough," Crosby said. "But I don't feel like every time I'm out there P.K.'s out there."

Nashville won Game 4 to even up the Stanley Cup Final at two games apiece. But in Game 5, Crosby got his payback.

Late in the first period, Subban brought the puck up the ice and passed it toward the front of the Penguins' net. Then he tangled with Crosby behind the net. Subban grabbed Crosby's stick, and the men hit the ice with Crosby on top. Crosby shoved his glove into Subban's face—it's what hockey players call a face wash. Crosby also banged Subban's head into the ice a few times for good measure. Both men were given two-minute penalties for holding.

Pittsburgh won the game easily, 6–0. And in Game 6, the Penguins won 2–0 to claim their second consecutive Stanley Cup. It was a tough defeat for Subban. And his night wasn't over yet.

In one of hockey's greatest traditions, each team shakes hands at the end of a series. That meant Subban and Crosby, both Canadians and former Olympic teammates, shook hands at the end of their battle. Crosby then skated off to celebrate with his teammates, while Subban went to a quiet Predators locker room.

Subban holds Crosby by the head during Game 5 of the 2017 Stanley Cup Final.

Despite the loss, Subban was seen as a hero in Nashville for standing up to Crosby. But in Pittsburgh and other cities, many people thought Subban was trying to make the Stanley Cup Final all about himself. Reporters asked Subban what he thought about the situation.

"I could probably answer the question if I knew why I'd be labeled as a villain," Subban said. "I don't know what I've done particularly wrong. I don't really focus on that. It's a lot of noise. I just choose not to listen to a lot of it. That's seemed to help me throughout my career."

Subban's ability to focus on hockey while enjoying himself has helped him become a star in the National Hockey League (NHL). By the age of 29, he was a three-time finalist for the Norris Trophy, which is given to the NHL's best defenseman. He won the award for the 2012–13 season, back when he was playing for the Montreal Canadiens.

No matter what jersey Subban wears, he is popular with fans. His No. 76 was one of the biggest sellers during the 2017 playoffs. Fans connect with Subban and his enthusiasm for the game. And Subban sees that as good for the league.

"In my opinion, this is the new NHL," Subban said at the 2016 All-Star Game. "That's the game now. Fans want to be able to interact with players and get to know them."

Subban has built himself quite a life. He's charitable. He travels the world. And yes, he promotes himself at times. In a sport where players usually blend in by not speaking too colorfully, Subban is not like most other players.

> "I don't know what I've done particularly wrong. I don't really focus on that. It's a lot of noise. I just choose not to listen to a lot of it. That's seemed to help me throughout my career."
>
> **– P.K. SUBBAN**

"There is a culture to the sport that I want to see respected and I don't want to see change," Subban says. "You want to respect the jersey, you want to respect the logo, you want to respect your players. But be yourself! Have fun."

P.K. Subban's parents, Karl and Maria, both moved to Canada when they were children.

CHAPTER 2
GROWING UP CANADIAN

P.K. Subban stands out in the NHL for many reasons, but perhaps the most obvious is his skin color. Subban is black, and he grew up in a country where a large majority of the population is white.

Both of Subban's parents are originally from the Caribbean. His father, Karl, was born in Jamaica, while his mother, Maria, was born on the island of Montserrat. In 1970, when Karl was 12 years old, he moved to Canada with his parents. Maria and her family moved to Canada that same year, but to a different city.

Karl used hockey as a way to settle into his new home of Sudbury, Ontario. He was one of the few black kids in the neighborhood. In an effort to fit in, Karl played hockey and watched *Hockey Night in Canada* on TV every Saturday night. He also became a big fan of the Montreal Canadiens, one of the Original Six teams in the NHL.

"We looked a bit different, but it wasn't really a problem because there I was playing hockey with all these kids," Karl said. "Hockey took us off the sidelines of being new Canadians and helped us become Canadians."

Karl and Maria eventually met, fell in love, and moved to Toronto so that Karl could begin his career as a teacher. Soon they started a family. First came two daughters, Nastassia and Natasha.

Pernell-Karl, known as P.K., arrived on May 13, 1989. When he was only four years old, he already knew what he wanted to do in life. Wearing pajamas

> "We looked a bit different, but it wasn't really a problem because there I was playing hockey with all these kids. Hockey took us off the sidelines of being new Canadians and helped us become Canadians."
>
> – KARL SUBBAN

and watching hockey on television, P.K. told his father that he wanted to be "one of those guys on TV."

P.K. first hit the ice wearing the skates of one of his sisters. Once he could skate well enough, his father signed him up for a house league. In a house league, players sign up at an ice rink, and parents pay a fee for them to play. Children are separated into teams based on age, and P.K. wound up playing with boys two or three years older than he was.

Figuring out how to put on hockey equipment proved to be a new challenge. Karl had played street hockey, but when he arrived at P.K.'s first ice hockey game he didn't know where each piece of equipment went. Karl had a bag filled with equipment donated by coworkers. The night before P.K.'s first official game, Karl tried to help his son put everything on. But Karl couldn't figure out some of the straps, so he watched how others put on the equipment in the locker room before the game.

P.K. showed promise, but Karl knew his son had to practice skating every day if he was going to succeed as a hockey player. So he took P.K. for late-night skating sessions after his job at a night school. P.K. would go to sleep in his outdoor clothes waiting for his father to return from work. By ten o'clock, his father would wake him up and drive him to Nathan Phillips Square in downtown Toronto. The square's reflecting pool became an outdoor rink once the weather was cold enough for the water to freeze.

P.K. played shinny—a form of hockey with no real rules, positions, or even goaltenders to protect the nets. He would skate and play until one o'clock in the morning with older children and even some adults. Then he and his father would head home. P.K. slept late each morning, since his kindergarten classes were in the afternoon.

All that practice helped P.K. improve his skating and learn how to play the game. He also worked on stickhandling and shooting by practicing in the basement.

In 1993, the Subbans moved to a house with a big backyard. Karl built a 30-foot by 30-foot ice rink each winter. That meant P.K. and his siblings could practice as much as they wanted.

Karl also knew the schedules of all the area's ice rinks. So if the weather stopped the Subbans from skating in their own backyard, Karl would drive his children to skate somewhere every day.

Skaters enjoy an afternoon at Toronto's Nathan Phillips Square, where Subban often practiced hockey as a child.

"That was our mindset all along—to be better," Karl wrote.

When P.K. was just five years old, his father enrolled him in another house league. Thanks to all the practice he'd put in, P.K. earned a spot on the six-year-old all-star team. He scored 19 of his team's 21 goals that season. People started to question how old he really was. P.K. looked bigger than his age because his father had bought oversized hockey equipment. That way, P.K. could use the gear longer before growing out of it. His father also wanted to be able to use the gear for P.K.'s younger brothers, Malcolm and Jordan.

P.K. also appeared older simply because he skated and played better than his peers. When P.K. was six, his father moved him to a select team. There, P.K. played with an all-star team for eight-year-olds.

"We didn't find out until the end of the season that he was not allowed to play two years ahead," Karl wrote.

P.K. kept working his way up through the house leagues. He first met coach Martin Ross, who ran the Toronto Professional Hockey School, when he was seven. One of the biggest lessons P.K. learned from Ross was that players should have fun.

One advantage P.K. had was being the oldest of three sons. That meant he got first crack at wearing the hockey gear, including a pair of hockey pants that his father won at a raffle.

"I guess I was in the best place being the first brother,"

"We didn't find out until the end of the season that (P.K.) was not allowed to play two years ahead."

– KARL SUBBAN

P.K. said. "So a lot of the stuff I got was brand new. My brothers, not so much."

As P.K. grew older, he worked his way up through the ranks. At the age of 14, he joined the North York Rangers bantam team in the Greater Toronto Hockey League. A year later, he moved to the Greater Toronto Hockey League's minor midget level with the Markham Islanders, where many NHL stars played on their way to hockey's top league.

It wasn't long before P.K. showed that he was ready for the next level.

MARKHAM ISLANDERS

Founded in 1979 by Jerry and Sylvia Jacobs, the Islanders play in the Greater Toronto Hockey League. The league was founded in 1911 to help children in Toronto develop their skills.

P.K. Subban played one season with Markham in 2004–05. He scored 43 points in 67 games.

**Subban warms up before a game with the OHL's
Belleville Bulls.**

CHAPTER 3
JUNIOR HOCKEY STAR

For years, P.K. Subban's parents had paid for him to be part of a hockey team. Now P.K. had a chance at being paid to play the game he loved. He was just shy of his 16th birthday when he entered the draft for the Ontario Hockey League (OHL). This junior league is for players between the ages of 16 and 21.

Players in the OHL move away from home to the town where their new team is based. They live with billet families, which are families that provide them with a home away from home. Players also can be paid a stipend to help with meals and entertainment. Another benefit of junior hockey is that players don't have to pay for their own equipment.

When draft day arrived, P.K. waited. And waited. Round after round went by, and it started to feel as if he wouldn't be selected. But finally, the Belleville Bulls chose him in the sixth round. When it was time to pick a jersey number, P.K. decided to wear No. 6. He wanted a constant reminder of how late in the draft he'd been chosen—and more motivation to prove everyone wrong.

George Burnett, Belleville's general manager and coach, believed in P.K.'s potential.

BELLEVILLE BULLS

The major junior hockey team was founded in 1979 and joined the Ontario Hockey League in 1981 as an expansion franchise. The Bulls played in Belleville, Ontario, through the 2014–15 season. Then they moved to Hamilton, Ontario, and were renamed the Hamilton Bulldogs. At that time, they became an American Hockey League franchise. That team was sold to the Montreal Canadiens and moved to St. John's, Newfoundland, for the 2015–16 season.

P.K. Subban was drafted in the sixth round by Belleville in 2005. He played four seasons with the Bulls starting with the 2005–06 season through 2008–09.

"He really helped to smooth P.K. out as a person," Karl Subban said of Burnett.

P.K. had played both forward and defense in his early years, but by the time he reached the OHL he had settled into his role as a defenseman. His first season in junior hockey didn't offer a sign of his future success as a scorer. He had only five goals and seven assists, ranking him 75th among defensemen in scoring.

P.K.'s game quickly improved as he grew bigger and stronger. In his second season, he was one of the best scoring defensemen in the OHL. He also tied for the team lead in games played, with 68. With Subban playing and scoring so much, the Belleville Bulls reached the OHL's Eastern Conference finals—the first of three straight berths.

Subban had proven himself as one of the best players his age. After having to wait until the sixth round of the OHL draft, he ended up going in the second round of the 2007 NHL Entry Draft. Scouts liked Subban's ability to skate fast up the ice while bringing the puck up on his stick. He also stood out for being able to shoot the puck and smother opponents. Scouts saw Subban as having the potential to be an elite defenseman, even if he was a bit flashy.

The Montreal Canadiens selected him 43rd overall. That meant he could soon be playing for his father's favorite team. Ever confident, Subban shook hands with Montreal executives at the draft. He had a message for them: "You guys made the right choice."

Most players who are drafted at the age of 18 still need to develop their skills in college or in the junior leagues. Subban was no exception. He returned to Belleville for another season with the Bulls in the OHL. But he made his next big jump later in 2007 by being named to Canada's world junior team.

The World Junior Championship is a major tournament for players who are 20 and younger. The event is often a proving ground for the NHL stars of tomorrow. Playing on that stage, Subban took part in seven games. However, he mostly sat on the bench as Canada won the gold in Sweden. Even so, Subban knew the experience was important because he could learn by watching.

"It is part of growing and maturing," Subban said. "You have to be

Subban was all smiles after the Montreal Canadiens drafted him in 2007.

patient. I relished the moments being there with great players."

When he made Canada's national junior team for 2008–09, Subban showed just how much he had learned. He was almost fully grown by then, at 5 feet

11 inches. He was also one of only four players to return from the previous year.

Subban was given the "A" as an alternate captain. That year's tournament was where people really started to notice his enthusiasm and flare. He was already trying to get people to use his preferred nickname, "the Subbanator." For people who didn't want to use that name, he suggested they call him P.K. instead of Pernell-Karl.

Subban made quite an impression on the ice. He had plenty of chances to score, too. In six games, Subban scored three goals with six assists as Canada won gold yet again. Canada coach Pat Quinn called him "Subbie-doo" in honor of Subban's spinning move around opposing players.

"Pat Quinn is a great coach, and he lets us get away with a few things," Subban said. "It is something that I may want to tone down a bit on this world stage."

The 2008–09 season was Subban's fourth and final year with the Bulls. He helped Belleville to a third straight Eastern Conference final. Subban left as the Bulls' all-time career scorer for a defenseman, with 190 points.

Two weeks after his last game with Belleville, Subban signed his first professional contract with a three-year, entry-level deal. That type of contract allows an NHL team to put a player in its minor league system and call him up to the major league whenever he's ready. The Canadiens sent Subban to the Hamilton Bulldogs in the American Hockey League (AHL).

> **"Pat Quinn is a great coach, and he lets us get away with a few things. It is something that I may want to tone down a bit on this world stage."**
>
> **– P.K. SUBBAN**

Subban spent only one season with the Bulldogs. In 77 games during the 2009–10 season, he set franchise records for a defenseman, with 18 goals and 53 points. Subban played so well that he was named both a First-Team AHL All-Star and a member of the AHL All-Rookie team. He also represented the Bulldogs at the 2010 AHL All-Star Game and won the AHL President's Award for his amazing season.

In fact, Subban played so well in the AHL that the Canadiens called him up in early 2010. He made a splash in his NHL debut, with an assist to go along with three shots on goal. Subban had another assist in his next game before being sent back to Hamilton.

The Canadiens called him up again during the playoffs, with the team facing elimination. Montreal was trailing three games to two in the first-round series against the Washington Capitals. With the series back in Montreal, Subban joined the Canadiens for Game 6. Subban had an assist in his NHL playoff debut and then helped Montreal win Game 7 to advance to the next round.

Subban stuck around for the rest of the postseason as Montreal beat Pittsburgh in seven games to reach the Eastern Conference finals. There the Canadiens fell short against the Philadelphia Flyers in five games.

HAMILTON BULLDOGS

Founded in 1996, the Bulldogs play in the American Hockey League, a minor professional hockey league affiliated with the NHL. The Bulldogs play in Hamilton, Ontario.

P.K. Subban played one season with the Bulldogs. He scored 53 points in 77 games.

Subban skates with the puck during a 2010 NHL playoff game against the Flyers.

Subban finished his first NHL postseason having played 14 postseason games and scored eight points as a rookie.

The Canadiens then sent Subban back to Hamilton in time for Game 7 of the AHL's Western Conference final. Unfortunately, the Bulldogs lost the game 4–2.

That was the last time Subban would play for the Bulldogs. The talented defenseman had shown that he was ready for the NHL.

Subban crashes into Ryan Malone of the Tampa Bay Lightning early in the 2010–11 season.

CHAPTER 4
WELCOME TO THE NHL

Thanks to his performance in the 2010 playoffs, P.K. Subban went to training camp that fall as a shoo-in to make the team and play for the Montreal Canadiens full time. He made a strong impression during his rookie season, scoring 38 points to rank third in the league for points by a rookie defenseman. Subban showed his knack for scoring at the right time with three game-winning goals. Only five defensemen in the entire NHL had more than Subban that season.

Subban even notched a hat trick in a win over the Minnesota Wild. He had never scored three goals in the same game in junior hockey. But he became the first Montreal rookie defenseman ever to accomplish the feat.

"I never thought in a million years that I would get a hat trick in an NHL game," Subban said after the game. "It's quite the thrill, it's something you dream about. To be able to do it this early in my career, it's a great feeling. Everything was going our way. The bounces went my way. The team did a great job creating the chances for me."

Canadiens fans were thrilled. But not everyone liked how Subban played. As a rookie that first full season, Subban didn't back down from hitting opponents or throwing his body into someone.

Some observers saw Subban's style as disrespectful to other players or to the game itself. Usually, rookies are expected to let their play on the ice speak for itself. Trash talk is only expected from players who have more experience. Subban didn't see things that way. He liked to talk, no matter how big a star his opponent might be.

"I never thought in a million years that I would get a hat trick in an NHL game. It's quite the thrill, it's something you dream about."

– P.K. SUBBAN

"You can't come in here as a rookie and play like that," Philadelphia captain Mike Richards told an interviewer in November 2010. "It's not the way to get respect from other players around the league. Hopefully someone on their team addresses it, because, I'm not saying I'm going to do it, but something might happen to him if he continues to be that cocky."

Subban defended the way he played, saying he wasn't the only NHL player confident in his skills. "As long as my teammates and the coaching staff are happy with what I'm doing, I'm going to continue to do that," he said.

In his second season, Subban played in 81 of 82 games, showing plenty of durability. He wasn't quite as productive in scoring, with two fewer points than the previous season. But he gave a sign of how much better he could be with a major jump in his plus-minus rating. This statistic measures a player's impact on the game. If the

"You can't come in here as a rookie and play like that. It's not the way to get respect from other players around the league....Something might happen to him if he continues to be that cocky."

– MIKE RICHARDS
CAPTAIN, PHILADELPHIA FLYERS

player's team scores a goal while he's on the ice, the player gets plus-1. But if his team gives up a goal while he's on the ice, he gets minus-1. Subban finished his first full season at minus-8. In contrast, he finished his second season at plus-9.

Still, Subban rubbed some in Montreal the wrong way. For instance, he was late to a morning meeting on a game day. He also fought with some teammates during practices. Teammates went to the interim head coach, Randy Cunneyworth, after Subban was late and asked for the defenseman to be punished.

"Not the first time it'd happened," forward Erik Cole said. "He'd had a couple of free passes. Cunney said to just focus on the game. It made a lot of guys feel like P.K. could do no wrong. That can create an imbalance in the locker room."

A lockout by NHL owners delayed the start of the 2012–13 season. Instead of the usual 82 games, there were only 48. And when the season finally started, Subban wasn't with the team. He sat out training camp along with the first six games because he insisted on a new contract. Subban and the Canadiens eventually agreed to a two-year deal worth $5.75 million.

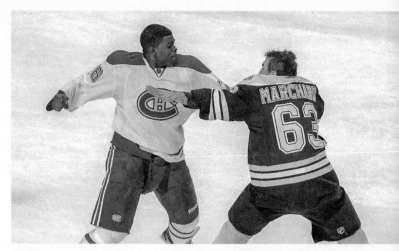

Subban dukes it out with Bruins winger Brad Marchand during a 2011 game in Boston.

Once he was back on the ice, Subban showed he was worth every penny. He scored 38 points—nearly one per game. Subban also cut down on penalties, spending less time in the box compared with the season before. Better yet, he played much better defensively. He had a plus-12 rating as he helped limit opposing teams from scoring when he was on the ice. Combined with his scoring, Subban earned the league's James Norris Memorial Trophy for the NHL's best defenseman in just his third season with Montreal.

"(With) these types of awards you have to give a lot of credit to your teammates because at the end of

Subban shows off his powerful slap shot against the Buffalo Sabres in early 2013.

the day those are the guys that are helping you and playing with you on the ice," Subban said when he won. "And I owe them a lot, especially coming into the season late. My teammates were amazing for me, and we've been great all year."

Subban played even better the next season, appearing in all 82 games for the first time in his career. He scored a career-high 53 points during the regular season. Subban also won an Olympic gold medal with Team Canada at the 2014 Winter Olympics. However, he played in only one Olympic game, a 6–0 victory over Austria in the preliminary round. Subban didn't sulk or complain about being a spectator at the Olympics, though, especially on such a star-studded roster.

"I'm walking away from this thing with a gold medal, and the reality is that everybody probably deserves to play, but as long as we win, I don't care," Subban said. "I don't think anybody in Canada cares. We're just happy we got the win and the gold medal."

Once the NHL's Olympic break ended, Subban improved again, especially in the playoffs. He helped Montreal sweep Tampa Bay before holding off Boston in seven games to reach the Eastern Conference finals. Montreal lost that series to the New York Rangers, but Subban scored 24 points in the Canadiens' 17 playoff games.

Despite his strong season, reaching an agreement on a new contract wasn't easy. Subban and the Canadiens went to arbitration. Each side made a case to a neutral person on how much he should be paid. The process had Montreal fans worried they would lose the star defenseman to another team.

A day before the ruling came down, Montreal and Subban agreed to a new contract. Subban signed an eight-year, $72 million deal that guaranteed him $9 million a year through the 2021–22 season.

"I've always felt strong about being a Montreal Canadien, and I never thought I would wind up anywhere else," Subban said after inking the new deal.

Along with the bigger paycheck, Subban also had a higher profile. He appeared on a TV show and talked about his diet—including how he drinks coffee before games to give him bad gas. It wasn't long before people around the NHL were talking about the comment. Kirk Muller, who had coached in Montreal during Subban's rookie season, could only laugh.

MONTREAL CANADIENS

Founded on December 4, 1909, the Canadiens are the only team in the NHL that was formed before the league was started in 1917. The Canadiens also are the only franchise to operate continuously throughout the NHL's history as one of the league's Original Six teams. Going into the 2018–19 season, the Canadiens have won 24 Stanley Cups.

P.K. Subban debuted in the NHL with Montreal during the 2009–10 season. He played six full seasons with Montreal, totaling 434 games through the 2015–16 season.

"(We'd) never heard anyone answer a question like that before," said Muller. "The only guy who would is P.K."

Armed with the new contract and even more popular with fans, Subban responded with his best season yet. He played all 82 games and scored a career-best 60 points, including a career-high 15 goals. He added eight more points in the playoffs before Montreal lost in the second round to Tampa Bay.

Subban enjoyed himself off the ice and away from hockey. But he angered some hockey traditionalists by drinking from a replica Stanley Cup at a benefit event. Subban avoided touching the Cup, which is a hockey no-no for any player who hasn't already won the sport's biggest trophy. He drank from the fake Cup using a straw.

Even though Subban talked a lot and lived a high-profile life as a member of Canada's biggest hockey team, he didn't say much on the topic of race despite being the Canadiens' lone black player.

In September 2015, Montreal let the players vote for captain after not having a captain the previous season. The top two candidates were Subban and Max Pacioretty. Montreal didn't announce a final tally, but

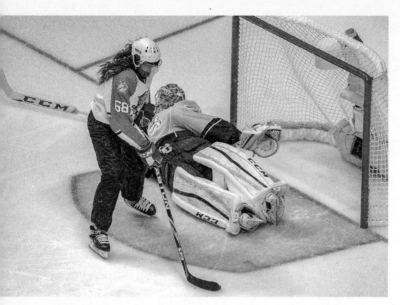

Subban wears a Jaromir Jagr jersey and a wig during the 2016 All-Star breakaway challenge.

Pacioretty was announced as the new captain. Subban was one of four alternate captains.

"The majority voted for Max," Montreal general manager Marc Bergevin said. "I won't go into details, but we didn't need to count twice."

That was only the start of the drama that season. Subban was voted to his first All-Star Game in January 2016. He had been a fan of hockey legend Jaromir Jagr—so during the skills competition, he came out in a Florida Panthers jersey with Jagr's number on it. He also imitated Jagr's famous flowing mullet. In a tribute that brought some fun to the event, Subban spray-painted a wig to look like Jagr's hair.

In February, Montreal coach Michel Therrien called out Subban for an error that led to a loss. With 2:17 left in a tie game against Colorado, Subban lost the puck and Colorado scored the game-winning goal.

"It was a selfish play that cost us the game," Therrien said. "The team worked hard. We deserved a better result. It's too bad an individual mistake cost us the game."

In March, Subban's season ended early due to an injury. During a game against Buffalo, Subban hurt his neck when he crashed into teammate Alexei Emelin. Subban was down on the ice for a few minutes before being put on a stretcher and taken to the hospital.

No one knew it at the time, but that was the last game Subban would play for the Montreal Canadiens.

> "It was a selfish play that cost us the game. The team worked hard. We deserved a better result. It's too bad an individual mistake cost us the game late in the game."
>
> **– MICHEL THERRIEN**
> COACH, MONTREAL CANADIENS

Subban meets a patient at the Montreal Children's Hospital in 2015.

CHAPTER 5
$10 MILLION COMMITMENT

P.K. Subban was disappointed when the Canadiens' season ended in May 2015. But the playoff loss meant the defenseman was free to attend a fundraiser for the Montreal Children's Hospital. And that set the stage for an amazing commitment by the young star.

Subban wanted to do more than just attend the fundraiser. He wanted to hold a live auction. So with only a week's planning, the event's schedule was changed to include the auction—something the organization had never done before.

At the fundraiser, Subban told attendees he would be selling a couple of his Canadiens jerseys for $1,000 apiece. But he actually brought 100 jerseys with him, and they all sold in five minutes. That meant Subban had raised $100,000 for the foundation.

"Actually, we didn't have enough of them," said Marie-Josée Gariépy, president of the hospital's foundation. "When you have an event with 600 people, you rarely see 100 people buying something that expensive. . . . He signed every jersey individually after and took a picture with every single donor that had purchased a jersey."

Subban wasn't done. He helped raise another $38,200 by auctioning off other items, including tickets to a game and an opportunity to meet him afterward.

Martin Ross, who had been Subban's youth hockey coach and was now his personal manager, went to the event too. Ross informed Gariépy that Subban wanted to talk to her when the fundraiser was over. He said Subban was looking for a charity to help.

Gariépy and Subban spoke for 90 minutes. Subban explained that he was thinking about making a large donation to the hospital. Gariépy then asked if he wanted his name to be displayed somewhere in the building to acknowledge his donation. One possibility was the hospital's atrium, a large entrance at the back of the building. Subban asked what the price tag would be to have such a prominent space named in his honor. Gariépy said it would require a donation of $10 million.

Subban spent the summer thinking about the opportunity. He had seen just how effective he could be attracting money for the hospital thanks to his work at the fundraiser. He also had some personal motivation that made him want to help. A few years earlier, Subban had met a young boy named Alex who had cancer. Subban became close not only with Alex but also with the boy's parents and family. Subban was in touch with Alex until he died.

"For me, that made me want to give back in a different way and really have a significant impact," Subban said. "And not just give back where everyone could say, 'Wow, that's great,' but give back where I could actually make a difference."

Subban says Alex lives on through everything he does to help other people, and that is why he focused his attention on children.

"The reality of it is that I want to help as many kids as I can," Subban said.

So in September 2015, at the age of 26, Subban announced his commitment to raise $10 million over a period of seven years for the Montreal Children's

La Fondation de l'Hôpital de Montréal pour enfants

The Montreal Children's Hospital Foundation

16 septembre 2015

10 000 000 $

Dix millions de dollars

P.K. SUBBAN

Merci ! Thank you!

Subban presents his pledge to raise $10 million for the Montreal Children's Hospital.

Hospital. To fulfill that pledge, he promised to give some of his own money and use the attention that comes with being an NHL star. After Subban's pledge, the hospital announced that its atrium would now be called the P.K. Subban Atrium.

"That gift has been transformational for all kinds of reasons," Gariépy said. "The money of course, because we're talking about a lot of money, but it's also P.K. himself. His brand, his personality, what he's bringing to the kids as an amazing role model. Every time he shows up, I'm telling you, people are so excited to see him, and he's happy."

Subban said he needed to take advantage of his opportunity while he had people's attention in the prime of his career.

"I have the ability as of right now to encourage other people to get involved," Subban said. "I may not always have that ability to get people to donate money and join my charity or my foundation or my events. But right now I do, so I'm trying to capitalize on that. Who knows? Hopefully I have that for the rest of my life, but why not do it now?"

With the donation, Subban also became a spokesman for the hospital foundation's board. His commitment was about more than just money. It resulted in stories that brought worldwide attention to the hospital. In fact, the hospital called it the largest donation by a professional athlete in Canadian history.

Part of Subban's commitment includes a fund called P.K.'s Helping Hand, which assists families that are struggling with sick children. A year into the commitment, Subban had raised $1.4 million and helped more than 9,000 families.

But he has given more than just money.

Subban speaks to a crowd from the hospital atrium that bears his name.

Subban challenged Canadians to record themselves singing "Jingle Bells" to help children in hospitals around Canada. Prime Minister Justin Trudeau took him up on that challenge, singing in both English and French.

Subban followed up by throwing a big Christmas party for children at the hospital, turning the atrium into a winter wonderland. Subban showed up to the party dressed in footie pajamas.

Seeing their son's commitment to helping children was no surprise to Subban's parents. His mother had raised him to always think of others. She had seen him give away his lunch at school to children who didn't have food.

And Subban's parents have made it clear that his commitment to the Montreal Children's Hospital will be the best thing their son gets out of hockey.

"Whenever you're able to use your success and achievement to help others, that is the best experience you can have in life," Karl Subban said. "It's great to be in the NHL. You're making money. You're in the bright lights. But now he's using it to help others. That's the ultimate."

That is why P.K. Subban sees hockey as something that he does now, not something that will last forever. He wants to be remembered for something much more than a sport.

"That's how I live my life," Subban said.

"Whenever you're able to use your success and achievement to help others, that is the best experience you can have in life. It's great to be in the NHL. You're making money. You're in the bright lights. But now he's using it to help others. That's the ultimate."

– KARL SUBBAN

Canadiens general manager Marc Bergevin discusses the blockbuster trade in June 2016.

CHAPTER 6
THE TRADE

In the summer of 2016, P.K. Subban's father, Karl, was about to take a walk with a friend. Then his daughter Natasha called with stunning news: the Montreal Canadiens had traded P.K. to the Nashville Predators.

"But you know P.K., we just thought he was joking around," Karl said. "After a couple of seconds of digesting it, I said, 'Let me check online.'"

Karl quickly learned that Natasha was right. Montreal, the team Karl had loved since moving to Canada as a child, had traded his son. It was one of the biggest deals in the history of the NHL, with one superstar defenseman traded for another. Subban was heading to Nashville, and Shea Weber would become a Canadien. The trade stunned the entire league, sparking headlines across the sports world.

In the days before the trade was announced, Canadiens general manager Marc Bergevin had been facing rumors that Montreal was looking to trade Subban. For instance, when Bergevin appeared at the NHL Entry Draft in Buffalo, New York, reporters mostly asked him about Subban. That's because Subban's contract had a clause that was about to take effect. It said the Canadiens would have to get Subban's approval before trading him to another team. But the clause had not yet kicked in, which meant the Canadiens were still free to trade Subban without his approval.

Bergevin never denied that he might trade Subban. Instead he said, "I don't want to answer any more P.K. questions."

But on June 29, the trade went down. Montreal got Weber, a six-year captain of the Predators. Unlike the charismatic Subban, Weber was a man who let his play on the ice speak for itself. Meanwhile, Nashville was more than happy to take Subban. With his speed and offensive skills, he was a perfect fit for how the Predators liked to play hockey.

Shea Weber played 11 seasons in Nashville before being traded to Montreal.

Subban was on vacation in France when the deal was announced. He spoke to reporters by telephone shortly after the trade became official.

"With a lot of the chatter that kind of happened over the little while, I'm a firm believer where there's smoke there's fire," Subban said. "Obviously, it's a little bit surreal, but it happened."

The trade sent shock waves through the league, too. Subban and Weber were both NHL All-Stars, and both had been on the Olympic team that won gold for Canada in 2014. Hockey analysts debated which team had gotten the better deal in the trade. Weber was bigger at 6 feet 4 inches and 236 pounds. In contrast, Subban was 6 feet and 210 pounds. But Weber turned 31 a few weeks after the trade, making him nearly four years older than Subban, who was 27 at the time.

Weber is a native of Canada just like Subban. Weber's contract was even more costly than Subban's. Weber is also very polite and prefers to let his powerful slap shot do most of the talking.

Montreal has a strong focus on hockey tradition. After all, no team has won close to as many Stanley Cups as the Habs. With that tradition in mind, players are usually expected to keep a lower profile. Subban's personal style often seemed to clash with those ideals.

In contrast, the Predators saw Subban as a perfect fit for a team in a nontraditional hockey market. The Predators weren't founded until 1998. Known as Music City, Nashville was better known for country singers

Before the big trade, Weber and Subban had both competed in the hardest shot event during the 2016 All-Star skills competition.

than for hockey. The Predators now had a player whose name was familiar to casual sports fans—someone who would help sell tickets.

"In hockey operations, they will say, 'P.K. Subban is my favorite player,'" Nashville general manager David Poile said. "I'm sitting there going, 'Did you see that, did you see that?' I'm a general manager, but someday, I would like to be a fan. And this is a guy that I would pay money to see."

As popular as the trade was in Nashville, fans in Montreal were stunned to lose one of the most popular Canadiens. Angry fans compared trading away Subban to a 1995 deal that sent goaltender Patrick Roy to Colorado. And many fans weren't happy that management apparently couldn't get along with Subban, whose boisterous personality appeared to be a bad fit for the Canadiens' franchise.

Bergevin called the trade one of the toughest decisions he had ever made as general manager of Montreal.

"I understand that P.K. is popular, but what we got in return is an elite defenseman," Bergevin said.

One fan was so angry at Montreal trading away Subban that he spent approximately $20,000 for a full-page ad in the *Montreal Gazette* newspaper expressing his feelings. Dr. Charles Kowalski had been a

> **"I understand that P.K. is popular, but what we got in return is an elite defenseman."**
>
> **– MARC BERGEVIN**
> GM, MONTREAL CANADIENS

season-ticket holder with the Canadiens. However, he said he planned to attend only one game the next season: the game in which Subban played as a visitor with Nashville. Kowalski saw Subban as an amazing role model for his children.

"I think the loss of P.K. Subban from Montreal, the bigger issue than hockey is the loss of his presence in the city of Montreal and his cause of raising money for the Children's Hospital. This is more important than the game of hockey," Kowalski said.

Canadiens fans may not have been happy, but there was nothing they could do about it. Subban was moving to Nashville. And there would be plenty of major changes in his life. For starters, he would be living outside of Canada for the first time. Then, after training camp opened, he would have to get to know a new coach, a new arena, and new teammates.

Subban shared some of his feelings in a documentary. The film focused on the whirlwind four months between his last game in Montreal and finding a new home in Tennessee. Subban found it difficult— almost impossible—to figure out why Montreal didn't want him anymore.

"I've always fallen on the sword (for the Canadiens)," Subban said. "But how could I fall on this sword?"

The trade was just as tough for P.K.'s father. After all, Karl had been a Canadiens fan since he was a kid, and now his son had been traded away. Karl compared the news of the trade to taking a powerful slap shot from Weber, who had won the league's hardest shot contest. Despite the disappointment and confusion, Karl admired his son's decision to look forward to the new opportunities in Nashville.

"I want him to love his new team and love his new city the way he did with Montreal," Karl Subban said.

Knowing how much the Predators wanted Subban definitely helped ease those hurt emotions. He looked forward to being with a team that wanted him to simply be himself—on and off the ice.

"That's music to my ears," Subban said.

Even with Subban wearing a different team's sweater, the defenseman still had his fans in Montreal. When the Canadiens were ousted in the first round of the 2017 playoffs, a bar in

"I've always fallen on the sword (for the Canadiens). But how could I fall on this sword?"

– P.K. SUBBAN

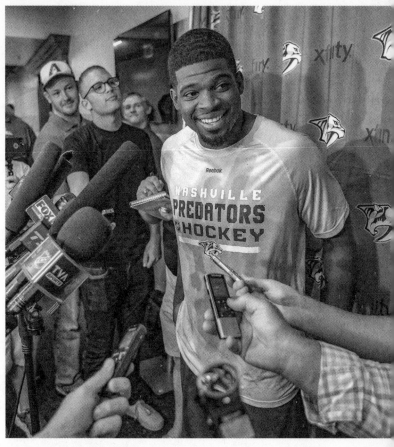

Subban chats with reporters after being traded to the Predators in 2016.

Montreal temporarily changed its name from Chez Serge to Chez Subban. Fans packed the bar to cheer Subban on through the Predators' run to the Stanley Cup Final.

Subban shows off his trademark celebration after scoring a goal against the Anaheim Ducks in 2017.

CHAPTER 7
A LONG LIST OF SKILLS

Shea Weber had been the Predators' captain, and he was a core piece of the franchise. So why was Nashville willing to trade him away? The answer was pretty simple: the Predators believed Subban was even better.

Calling Subban an offensive-minded defenseman almost undersells how good he is. He has scored so much that his celebration—dropping to a knee and pretending to shoot an arrow—is now seen as his trademark move.

Before joining the Predators, Subban had played at least 68 games each season (not counting the lockout-shortened season in 2012–13). In four of those six seasons, Subban scored at least 10 goals. And he was even better at setting up teammates.

Hockey is a game where teamwork matters. That's why each goal can receive up to two assists for the passes that lead to the scoring shot. Subban consistently showed that he could do just that. Starting with his first full season in the NHL, his assist numbers went up almost every year.

That made Subban a perfect fit for the way Nashville wanted to play hockey. The Predators liked the fact that he skated remarkably fast for a 210-pound player. That speed allowed him to play both offense and defense. In addition, Subban could keep the puck on his stick while skating, which was a big help when his team started an attack on the opponent's zone.

Subban's critics often say he tries to score more than he should. They argue that a defenseman should worry more about protecting his goaltender. And Subban's energetic, playful style on the ice seems to aggravate those critics even more. In fact, the Montreal Canadiens once ordered him to stop a post-game celebration known as the "triple low five." His coach wanted Subban to stick to the team's usual celebration

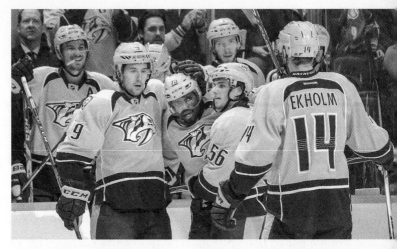

Subban's teammates congratulate him after he scored a goal for the Predators in 2016.

of skating to center ice and raising his stick up to the fans.

"It's a team concept," Canadiens coach Michel Therrien said. "You have to respect the game, the other team, and the fans."

But Subban was simply having too much fun on the ice not to celebrate.

For all his skill, Subban's best weapon might be his slap shot. That's where he pulls his stick back and then swings through the puck with power. The flying puck is painful for opponents to block, and it moves so quickly goalies have a hard time sliding over to stop it.

Subban also has great vision on the ice. He takes shots that few hockey players could see, let alone attempt.

"I don't do anything just because it looks good. I do it because it's going to get the job done," Subban said. "If I feel that putting a two-and-a-half foot saucer pass over some guy's stick (gives us) a scoring chance, that's what I'm going to do. Not every player has the skill or talent level to do that, but if you do, then yeah, you've got to use your skill or talent to execute, right? That's how I see it."

Subban is a defenseman, so it's no surprise that he can defend. He makes a living checking opponents and leaning on them so heavily that it's nearly impossible to find room for a shot. He also does whatever he can to get the other team thinking about something other than hockey. He even admitted to farting in

"I don't do anything just because it looks good. I do it because it's going to get the job done. If I feel that putting a two-and-a-half foot saucer pass over some guy's stick (gives us) a scoring chance, that's what I'm going to do. Not every player has the skill or talent level to do that."

- P.K. SUBBAN

front of the net in case that helps distract the goalie. He's also known for using his rear end to check opposing players into the boards, protecting his shoulders at the same time.

"You don't want to go through a dislocated shoulder, labrum surgery, that garbage," Subban said. "Your butt and back are two of the strongest parts of your body."

Subban's determination to annoy opposing players is part of the reason why some critics don't like him. In the 2014 Eastern Conference semifinals, Subban had the final goal in a 4–2 loss in Game 5 against Boston. Bruins enforcer Shawn Thornton squirted a water bottle at Subban's face as the defenseman skated with the puck past the Boston bench. Thornton was fined for his actions.

"From a Boston perspective, I'll say he's a dynamic player, agitating, very effective," Thornton said. "His antics are a little bit exaggerated. I'll also say he was the best player in the series."

> **"From a Boston perspective, I'll say he's a dynamic player, agitating, very effective."**
>
> **– SHAWN THORNTON**
> WINGER, BOSTON BRUINS

Subban makes a play during his debut with the Predators in 2016.

CHAPTER 8
HELLO, NASHVILLE!

P.K. Subban ended up being a perfect match for Nashville. Subban, with all his personal flair, was a natural fit in a city that understands the value of entertainment. Subban also fit the offensive scheme of Predators coach Peter Laviolette.

Some coaches prefer defensemen to hang back near the blue line, ready to retreat as soon as the puck moves toward their own end of the ice. But not Laviolette. He encourages his defensemen to chase the puck deep into the offensive zone and try to score whenever possible.

Subban seemed to be the final piece in the puzzle for Nashville. Predators fans hoped he would rev up the team's offense and help them go deeper in the playoffs than ever before.

When Subban arrived in Nashville, one of his first meetings was with the Predators' marketing department. Subban wanted to discuss ideas to promote the team. He also wanted to talk about the local charities he could work with. In the days that followed, Subban hung out with some of his new teammates and met with Laviolette to learn what his new coach expected from him.

Subban also made time to check out the entertainment options in downtown Nashville. One night, he took the stage at Tootsie's, a famous music venue near the Predators' arena. He fit right in, singing "Folsom Prison Blues" by country legend Johnny Cash.

It didn't take long for Subban's parents to stop worrying about how their son was adapting to his new home.

"They've really accepted him well, and he feels really good about it," his mother said.

When Subban hit the ice in his first game with the Predators, he couldn't have scripted a better start. Nashville was playing its biggest rival, the Chicago

Subban and Predators GM David Poile hold a news conference shortly after Subban joined the team.

Blackhawks, in the season opener. And Subban scored a goal on his first shot, helping his team to a 3–2 win.

When the Canadiens visited Nashville in January 2017, an injury forced Subban to miss the game. Understandably, he was frustrated that he wouldn't be able to compete against his old team. Subban wound up missing 16 games with the injury. Fortunately, he healed in time for the Predators' trip to Montreal's Bell Centre two months later.

The Canadiens honored Subban with a video tribute before the game. The defenseman had tears running down his cheeks as fans chanted "P.K.! P.K.!"

Once the game started, Subban found himself booed when he assisted on a goal that put Nashville up 1–0. Canadiens fans went home happy, though, as Montreal won 2–1. Despite the loss, Subban enjoyed himself.

"It was great," Subban said. "That's the first time I've ever been booed at the Bell Centre. I enjoyed that."

The Predators had their ups and downs during the 2016–17 season, and they scraped into the playoffs as the last team in. Now Subban was ready to prove that his team belonged there.

However, his reputation came along with him.

In a second-round game, St. Louis Blues defenseman Joel Edmundson knocked Subban's helmet off. Edmundson was sent to the penalty box, but Subban was also penalized for trying to make the hit look worse than it was. The NHL fined Subban $2,000 for the dive, noting that he'd received a warning for a similar incident earlier in the year.

"That's the first time I've ever been booed at the Bell Centre. I enjoyed that."

– P.K. SUBBAN

Despite the theatrics, Subban scored 10 points in the first three rounds of the playoffs. His tenacious play helped the Predators win their first Western Conference championship in team history. Nashville was now competing for the Stanley Cup against the defending champion Pittsburgh Penguins.

The Predators played tough in the series, but they ended up losing to the Penguins in six games. It was a hard pill to swallow for Subban. Even so, he was determined to show that his first season in Nashville was just a preview of good things to come.

During the 2017–18 regular season, Subban anchored one of the best defenses in the NHL. Subban himself scored a career-high 16 goals. That made him fourth in the NHL among defensemen. He also played in all 82 games for the third time in his career.

For a second straight year, fans voted Subban captain of the Central Division for the All-Star Game. Subban was so popular that he received more votes than any other player from the NHL's Central Division.

Thanks in large part to Subban's fantastic season, the Predators won their first Presidents' Trophy. That award goes to the team with the best record in the league. Nashville also won its first Central Division title. Going into the 2018 playoffs, Predators fans thought it was finally their year to win the Stanley Cup.

Fans of the other teams in the league seemed to dislike Subban more than ever. During a first-round playoff series, Colorado fans were furious when Subban punched Avalanche center Nathan MacKinnon in the back of the head. The boos rained down even more heavily when no penalty was called.

The Predators took care of Colorado in six games. In the next round, they faced the division-rival Winnipeg Jets. From the moment Subban stepped onto the Winnipeg ice during warm-ups, fans booed him. And throughout the series, they made Subban a top target of their attention.

After a Game 5 loss put Nashville on the verge of elimination, Subban spoke up. He promised that the Predators would win Game 6 in Winnipeg and bring the series back to Nashville for Game 7.

"Every single guy in here believes that," Subban said.

The Predators routed the Jets 4–0. After the game, Subban said he only shared what all his teammates were thinking. Goalie Pekka Rinne agreed with him.

Subban levels a Blues player during a 2017 playoff game.

"Obviously, I feel like it's nice that somebody says it out loud," Rinne said.

Unfortunately, things didn't go Nashville's way in Game 7. The Predators wound up losing by a score of 5–1. Subban scored the lone goal for his team on a big slap shot. He also played the most minutes of any player on either team, with over 28 minutes on the ice. At one point in the game, he was yelling at his teammates on the bench trying to rally them.

After the game, a guest on a Canadian radio show suggested that the Predators might trade Subban simply to get him off their team. Such a move would make sense for Subban's critics, who wondered if the defenseman had worn out his welcome in yet another locker room.

The Nashville coach quickly shot down that idea, saying the Predators were moving in a good direction with Subban on their team.

"He was just awesome in both years for me," Laviolette said. "He's coachable. Plays big minutes. Plays against the best players. Produces in the defensive zone and produces in the offensive zone. I mean, you can't ask for anything more than that."

Those words may have been nice to hear, but they weren't nearly enough for Subban. He met with

NASHVILLE PREDATORS

The Predators started play in October 1998 in Nashville, Tennessee, as an expansion franchise in the National Hockey League.

P.K. Subban joined the Predators via trade on June 29, 2016. In his first season with the team, Subban helped the Predators reach the Stanley Cup Final.

The Nashville crowd goes nuts after Subban scored a goal against the Jets during the 2018 playoffs.

reporters after the Predators' season ended—a season in which Nashville had been the favorite to win the Stanley Cup. Subban said the Predators had to learn how to be better. But mostly, he talked about how he himself needed to improve. Train harder, be better, and return to the Final.

Subban had high hopes for the future. Not just for himself, but for the game of hockey.

"I'm in the United States. . . . This is where the game needs to grow. If you want to do it, win a championship here and see what happens," Subban said. "We have the opportunity to do that. I'm pretty stoked, man."

Willie O'Ree played in 45 games for the Bruins over the course of his NHL career.

CHAPTER 9
BEING BLACK IN HOCKEY

The NHL's color barrier wasn't broken until 1958. That's when Boston Bruins winger Willie O'Ree became the league's first black player. But unlike the other major team sports, pro hockey hasn't seen many black players over the years. In fact, between 1958 and 2001, there were only 36 black players in the NHL.

In Canada, black people make up a small portion of the total population. According to the 2016 census, for example, only 3.5 percent of Canadians were black. That came out to just under 1.2 million people. In the 1990s, when Subban was growing up, the number was even lower.

When P.K. Subban and his younger brothers, Malcolm and Jordan, played hockey as children, they often found that they were the only black kids at the rink. Sometimes they heard racist insults as they played. The first time it happened, P.K. was about eight years old, playing in a tournament at the Vaughan Iceplex in Toronto. He came out of the dressing room crying. He told his parents a boy called him the N-word while on the ice.

His parents had never talked with their children about that word, because Karl Subban had never heard anyone use it toward him. The Subbans told P.K. not to cry—it was only a word, and it couldn't hurt him.

"There weren't too many kids playing hockey who looked like P.K., so I'm quite sure he knew he was different," Karl later wrote. "But now someone had communicated it to him in a way he didn't like."

Subban's parents taught him that giving any attention to racists could only distract him from his goal of playing in the NHL. So he learned to simply ignore such people. Subban's father believes focusing on the job at hand made his son better.

"If someone throws a banana on the ice, am I going to stop playing hockey? Come on," Karl wrote.

Subban continued to stay focused—all the way to the NHL. That focus was never tested more than after Montreal won a double-overtime playoff game over Boston in 2014. Subban scored two goals in the game, one of which was the winner in overtime. After the game, angry Boston fans started flooding social media with comments that Subban didn't belong in hockey. They used the hashtag #whitesonly.

> "There weren't too many kids playing hockey who looked like P.K., so I'm quite sure he knew he was different. But now someone had communicated it to him in a way he didn't like."
>
> **– KARL SUBBAN**

Some Boston fans defended Subban, whose brother Malcolm had been drafted by the Bruins in 2012. Malcolm, a goalie, was playing that season in the American Hockey League for the Bruins' top minor league team.

The Boston Bruins issued a statement saying the racist views had come from "an ignorant group of individuals" and did not reflect the beliefs of anyone connected to the team. A day later, several Bruins

Racist comments tested Subban's resolve during the 2014 playoffs.

players and head coach Claude Julien also condemned the hateful messages.

Subban did not comment on the matter until after the next game of the series. He defended the Bruins, saying Boston had a passionate fan base. He also said he knew the NHL or the Bruins would deal with the issue. As for Subban? He said he wanted to move on.

"You know what the funny thing is, is that we get stronger as a league. You see how people come together, and it's great," Subban said.

Subban was putting into action the lessons his parents had taught him: ignore the noise, and focus on hockey. It worked, too. Subban and the Canadiens got the last word when Montreal beat Boston in seven games to reach the conference final.

"I never look at myself as a black player," Subban said. "I think of myself as a hockey player who wants to be the best hockey player in the league. I know I'm black. Everyone knows I'm black. But I don't want to be defined as a black hockey player."

The number of black players in the NHL continues to expand. For instance, when Subban joined the Predators, the team already had Joel Ward and Seth Jones on its roster. Subban's brothers are part of that expansion, too. Malcolm Subban made his NHL debut in the 2014–15 season, playing one game for Boston. In 2017, the Vegas Golden Knights claimed Malcolm off

"I never look at myself as a black player. I think of myself as a hockey player who wants to be the best hockey player in the league. I know I'm black. Everyone knows I'm black. But I don't want to be defined as a black hockey player."

– P.K. SUBBAN

waivers, and he became the backup to goalie Marc-Andre Fleury.

Malcolm wound up winning six of the first eight games he started. Next up was a game against P.K. and the Predators. All those childhood games played in the backyard set the brothers up for an amazing night.

Before the game, P.K. and Malcolm got together with their father for photos on the ice. Karl was wearing a Vegas jersey and rooting for Malcolm. After all, Malcolm was five years younger than P.K. and had not yet established himself as an NHL star.

During the game, Nashville fans started their usual chant about how the opposing goalie stinks—even though the goalie shared the same name as their own star defenseman. At one point, P.K. even made eye contact with his younger brother during a face-off near the Vegas net.

At the end of regulation, the game was tied 3–3. No goals were scored in the overtime period, so the game came down to a shootout. That's when Malcolm showed what he could do. He stopped all six shots, giving the Golden Knights the victory.

Despite the Predators' loss, P.K. was proud of his little brother.

P.K. Subban (right) poses with his brother Malcolm (left) and his father (center) before a 2017 game between the Predators and the Golden Knights.

"It was awesome," P.K. said. "Obviously I don't like to see him play that well against us, but you know he played well, and I'm happy for him. It's been a rocky road to get to where he is now, but he's a pro now. You can see that. As a family, today's a big day."

P.K.'s youngest brother, Jordan, is a defenseman just like his big brother. Jordan was drafted by the Vancouver Canucks in 2013 and spent several years in the minors. Going into the 2018–19 season, he had not yet played in the NHL. But P.K. remained confident that his youngest brother would make it.

"I really do think he has a lot more potential than both myself and Malcolm," P.K. said.

Subban may downplay his race, but there's no denying he has benefitted from getting to know Willie O'Ree, the NHL's first black player. It has helped Subban learn just how far the league has come in regard to racism.

In February 2015, the two men sat down together for a television interview for Black History Month. O'Ree told Subban stories of what he dealt with during his playing days. For instance, fans sometimes threw things at him while he was in the penalty box. And on one occasion, an opponent called him a racial slur before knocking out a couple of his teeth.

"Racism in sports, even today, is still talked about so much," Subban said. "It comes in so many different forms that it's sometimes hard to tell when it's happening."

When football players started kneeling during the American national anthem in 2016 and 2017 to protest racial injustice, Subban took another approach. He said he would never kneel because of his respect for the American flag. The Predators decided as an organization not to protest during the anthem.

For Subban, the reason was simple. Yes, he's a black hockey player, but no one can control his or her skin color. Instead, Subban focused on being the best player in the NHL—and that was something he could control.

"That's how you're judged in this world, by what you do and your work ethic and your character," Subban said. "That's how I've been judged. . . . I'd like to hope that people aren't being judged by the color of their skin and their ethnic background."

"That's how you're judged in this world, by what you do and your work ethic and your character. That's how I've been judged. . . . I'd like to hope that people aren't being judged by the color of their skin and their ethnic background."

– P.K. SUBBAN

The Predators play at Bridgestone Arena, which is located in the heart of Nashville's famous entertainment district.

CHAPTER 10

HOLIDAY SURPRISES AND BLUELINE BUDDIES

Living in Nashville didn't end Subban's commitment to children. The change in scenery simply gave the big-hearted defenseman new opportunities to help people.

After surprising a group of young patients at a Nashville hospital, Subban gave them a day to remember. Wearing a top hat for the occasion, Subban started by loading the kids into a carriage for a tour of downtown Nashville. Next, he treated the kids to a shopping spree at the shop in the Predators' home arena. Then he capped off their big day by taking them to a private concert by country star Dierks Bentley.

With so much talk in the United States about national anthem protests and social injustice, Subban came up with his own approach to the situation. He said he supports athletes who exercise their right to protest, but he wanted to bring people together rather than driving them apart. With that in mind, he created a program called P.K.'s Blueline Buddies.

The idea of the program is to build bridges between underprivileged youth and the police officers who risk their lives every day. Subban buys tickets for each of Nashville's home games. He gives one ticket to a student in middle school or high school, and another ticket to a police officer.

When Subban was growing up in Toronto, he had friends who disliked the police because they had witnessed officers behaving inappropriately. And he knew that plenty of young people in Nashville felt the same way. Subban hoped an evening of hockey might help police officers and young people find common ground.

The Predators work with groups around Nashville to choose students for the program. Meanwhile,

Subban poses with a group that took part in the Blueline Buddies program in 2018.

the Nashville Police Department selects officers to participate. The student and officer start their evening by hanging out with Subban before the game and having dinner inside the arena. Then they watch the game from great seats. To top it off, they meet Subban again after the game. All of those activities are certainly fun, but the real point of the program is breaking down barriers by helping people get to know each other.

"I think this hopefully helps law enforcement feel they're appreciated. It's a delicate topic, but I think everything with this program is positive," Subban said.

Some of the people selected for the Blueline Buddies program are young men from the YWCA's MEND program. This group's goal is to end violence against women. Shan Foster, who runs MEND, called Subban's idea incredible for changing the conversation.

"This takes the politics out of it, takes away the negative perceptions society has right now. This is about the human side of all of us," Foster said.

Subban started the Blueline Buddies program during the 2017–18 season. While the Predators were wrapping up the regular season, the Nashville Police Department honored Subban and the team with its Community Service Award. Subban was on the road in Washington, DC, during the ceremony, so he couldn't accept the award in person. But Rebecca King, the team's director of community relations, accepted the award in his absence.

"It's a unique program that's really taken kind of a life of its own," King said. "It gives the officers a night out of entertainment, it gives the kids a night out of entertainment, but it's also got the underlying platform of bringing youth and officers together to see that not all kids are bad and not all officers are out to get them."

Some people might call that enough charity work, especially with a full-time job playing hockey. But not Subban. He went even bigger with his holiday surprise in December 2017.

Subban started off by disguising himself as an old man. Makeup artists covered his head to make him look mostly bald, and they gave him a big gray beard. Then Subban went out into the streets of Nashville, handing out candy canes and other surprises. He even gave one couple a free night at a hotel across from the Predators' arena.

Subban also had a special gift in store for a family connected to his Blueline Buddies program. A single mother of two boys had one wish for Christmas. She wanted a new living room with a couch and love seat. Subban helped make that dream come true. He delivered the furniture and helped set it up, along with

Subban and his parents share a moment with a patient at the Montreal Children's Hospital in 2017.

a Christmas tree and presents. But when Subban tried to surprise the family dressed as an old man, one of the boys immediately recognized him as the Predators defenseman. With help from Predators captain Roman Josi, Subban also brought in a nice rug, new dishes, and a microwave for the kitchen. Subban even hired a chef to cook dinner that night.

Subban hasn't forgotten his commitment to the Montreal Children's Hospital. He sent a big box filled with toys to the hospital as part of the surprise for his Christmas spirit–filled event. In August 2017, he also hosted a hockey clinic in Montreal that raised $50,000 for the hospital. Children got to skate with Subban and spend time with him off the ice as well.

Subban understands that timing matters. With the Predators in the 2018 playoffs, he had T-shirts made in Nashville's blue and gold colors, showing him celebrating and the words "P.K. APPROVED" on the front. The sale of the limited-edition shirts benefitted his foundation, giving his fans a way to represent the Predators and help sick children. The defenseman has made it clear that even though he doesn't play in Montreal anymore, his commitment to the hospital— and his promise to raise $10 million—would not waver.

"I choose, with some of the time that I have and the platform I have, to try to help as many people as I can," Subban said. "That's not something that just happened to me one day. That's the way my family has operated since I've come into this world. I'm just trying to follow in the same footsteps as my family members in any way that I can."

Subban sports a flashy suit on the red carpet during the 2018 NHL Awards.

CHAPTER 11
A MAN OF STYLE AND PRIVACY

P.K. Subban is a man who loves to look good, and he's easily the life of any party. His energy and charisma just seem to draw people in.

Subban knows that dressing for the occasion matters. Whether he's arriving on a red carpet for the NHL All-Star Game or going to a movie premiere with someone like director Spike Lee, Subban always shows up dressed stylishly. Growing up in the Subban family helped form his fashion sense. In addition, hockey is a sport where men are expected to dress up in suits.

"I was taught that when I leave my house, I have to look a certain way, and I think that's why I was drawn to suits," Subban said. "I always wanted to be taken seriously."

That's why Subban has had his own tailor for years. Subban then went a step further by designing his own collection of men's suits for a Canadian company. He even convinced his family members to take part in a photo shoot to promote the clothing line. His first line featured suits, shirts, belts, cuff links, tie bars, and hats. Now, people everywhere have the option of dressing from head to toe just like Subban.

"The one thing that I'll always maintain in terms of my style and fashion sense is to straddle the line as someone who is creative and fashion-forward but also someone who is classic, clean, and sharp," Subban said. "I want to reflect and respect what I represent, and that's the organization I play for and my family."

But Subban also likes to have fun. For his first Halloween after being traded to Nashville, he dressed up all in purple in honor of the musician Prince. Subban decked himself out in a purple overcoat with a puffy shirt. He even wore a curly wig to imitate Prince's famous hairstyle.

Subban called living in the American South a great experience for himself and his family, especially after growing up in Canada.

A well-dressed Subban family poses before the 2015 NHL Awards.

"Whether you're single or you're married with a family, it's an awesome place to live," Subban said. "I've really enjoyed it, and I know my family and friends have because I can't get them out of here. I can't get them out of my house."

Subban loves to eat, and he's a creature of habit. Wherever he lives, he finds a local restaurant and becomes a regular. He had his own table at a Montreal restaurant where he often picked up food to take with him on road trips. In Tennessee, a restaurant in a small town outside of Nashville keeps a corner spot open for Subban. The star defenseman even has a drink named after him.

"P.K. is just a normal guy who happens to be an amazing hockey player," restaurant owner Jason McConnell said.

Even those who aren't fans of Subban's flashy style have to admit that he's doing good work. Don Cherry, a former NHL coach and TV broadcaster in Canada, said he would like to see Subban tone down his goal celebration and showing off on the ice. Yet Cherry still remained a big fan of Subban.

"Don't get me wrong," Cherry said. "He's great for hockey. And, if you ever talk to him personally, he's the most polite, nicest kid. You'd want him for a son, you know what I mean?"

Subban may be impossible not to notice when he shows up at an

> "He's great for hockey. And, if you ever talk to him personally, he's the most polite, nicest kid. You'd want him for a son, you know what I mean?"
>
> **– DON CHERRY**
> CANADIAN TV BROADCASTER AND FORMER NHL COACH

NHL awards show wearing a red tuxedo jacket with black trim. And he is more than happy to talk about fashion, his charity work, or preparing for a big game. But as much as Subban talks on and off the ice, he's a bit more private about his personal life.

As a single and wealthy young man, Subban makes sure to enjoy his time off between the seasons. He has cruised around the Mediterranean Sea on vacation. He met former NBA star Magic Johnson while walking around Monaco in 2014. He became friends with tennis star Novak Djokovic in 2017, and he began dating champion skier Lindsey Vonn in 2018.

Subban's ability to attract people to him has also made him very popular with advertisers. He has had sponsorship deals with Samsung, Listerine, Gatorade, Air Canada, Adidas, and Bridgestone. Not even being traded away from Montreal could keep him off TV in that market. He pitched a local pizza restaurant in a TV commercial where he tipped the delivery driver with his new Predators jersey—all while speaking French.

The NFL's Tennessee Titans made sure to invite Subban to a game in 2016 to serve as the team's "12th Titan." The pregame honor includes grabbing a sword

Subban pumps up the crowd before a Tennessee Titans football game in 2016.

to drive into the ground. Subban seized the moment to pour water over himself before ripping off his shirt and waving it over his head.

"I don't think I ever imagined taking my shirt off in front of 70,000 people," Subban said.

Subban is so popular that EA Sports put him on the cover of the *NHL 19* video game.

Through it all, Subban uses a positive attitude in everything he does. Credit the lessons taught to him by his parents and the experience of seeing how that always works out for the best.

"I really believe that a lot of the outcome of whatever situation you're in is determined by your attitude," Subban said. "For me, I always approach everything with a positive attitude. I seem to get more success doing that than anything else."

That approach sure seems to have paid off.

"I really believe that a lot of the outcome of whatever situation you're in is determined by your attitude. For me, I always approach everything with a positive attitude. I seem to get more success doing that than anything else."

— P.K. SUBBAN

TIMELINE

1989

Pernell-Karl Subban is born in Toronto, Ontario, on May 13.

2005

Subban is drafted by the Belleville Bulls of the Ontario Hockey League in the sixth round, at No. 105 overall.

2007

The Montreal Canadiens draft Subban at No. 43 overall in the NHL Entry Draft.

2010

Subban makes his NHL debut on February 12 in a game at Philadelphia.

2013

Subban wins the Norris Trophy, which is awarded to the NHL's top defenseman.

2014

Subban agrees to an eight-year, $72 million contract with Montreal.

2015

Subban commits to raising $10 million for the Montreal Children's Hospital.

2016

In a trade that stuns the hockey world, Montreal sends Subban to Nashville in exchange for Shea Weber.

2017

Subban plays in the Stanley Cup Final for the first time in his career.

2018

Subban is a finalist for the Norris Trophy and King Clancy Memorial Trophy. He also appears on the cover of the *NHL 19* video game.

FACT SHEET

- **Name:** Pernell-Karl Subban
- **Born:** May 13, 1989, in Toronto, Ontario
- **Height:** 6 feet
- **Weight:** 210 pounds
- **Position:** right-handed defenseman
- **Minor league team:** Hamilton Bulldogs (2009–2010)
- **NHL teams:** Montreal Canadiens (2009–2016); Nashville Predators (2016–)

BY THE NUMBERS

- **NHL games played:** 582
- **NHL goals scored:** 89
- **NHL assists:** 288
- **NHL career points:** 377
- **NHL career playoff games:** 90
- **NHL career playoff goals:** 17
- **NHL career playoff assists:** 42
- **NHL career playoff points:** 59

Accurate through the 2017–18 season

CAREER AWARDS

- **World Junior Championships gold medal:** 2008, 2009
- **Winter Olympics gold medal:** 2014
- **Norris Trophy:** 2013
- **NHL All-Star:** 2016, 2017, 2018
- **Central Division captain at NHL All-Star Game:** 2017, 2018

FAMILY

- **Father:** Karl Subban
- **Mother:** Maria Subban
- **Sisters:** Nastassia and Natasha
- **Brothers:** Malcolm and Jordan
- **Malcolm Subban:** Born December 21, 1993. Drafted No. 24 overall in the first round by the Boston Bruins in 2012. Claimed off waivers by the Vegas Golden Knights on October 3, 2017.
- **Jordan Subban:** Born March 3, 1995. Drafted No. 115 overall as the 24th pick in the fourth round of the 2013 draft by the Vancouver Canucks. Traded to Los Angeles for Nic Dodd in 2017. Signed as a free agent by Toronto in 2018.

FOR MORE INFORMATION

BOOKS

Lozano, Claryssa. *Nashville Predators*. New York: AV2 by Weigl, 2015.

Mortillaro, Nicole. *Willie O'Ree: The Story of the First Black Player in the NHL*. Toronto: James Lorimer & Company, 2018.

Peters, Chris. *Hockey Season Ticket: The Ultimate Fan Guide*. Mendota Heights, MN: Press Room Editions, 2018.

WEBSITES

Nashville Predators
www.nhl.com/predators

National Hockey League
www.nhl.com

P.K. Subban: Official Website
www.pksubban.com

PLACES TO VISIT

BELL CENTRE

1909, avenue des Canadiens-de-Montréal
Montreal, QC H4B 5G0
514-932-2582
www.centrebell.ca

Holding more than 21,000 Canadiens fans, Subban's former home in Montreal is the largest arena in the NHL. Take a look at the rafters, and admire the banners from Montreal's many Stanley Cup wins.

BRIDGESTONE ARENA

501 Broadway
Nashville, TN 37203
615-770-2000
www.bridgestonearena.com

The best place to see Subban play hockey is in front of a screaming crowd of Predators fans. The arena opened in 1996, two years before the Predators were formed.

SELECT BIBLIOGRAPHY

Basu, Arpon. "Playoff Loss Led Subban to Become Hospital
  Benefactor." *NHL*, 24 Dec. 2015, www.nhl.com/news/playoff-
  loss-led-subban-to-become-hospital-benefactor/c-794107.

Bittner, Adam. "P.K. Subban: Sidney Crosby Thinks I Have
  Bad Breath." *Pittsburgh Post-Gazette*, 3 June 2017, www.
  post-gazette.com/sports/penguins/2017/06/04/predators-
  Subban-penguins-stanley-cup-final-Sidney-Crosby/
  stories/201706040177.

Colby, Scott. "How P.K. Subban's Dad Prepared Him for the Game
  of Life." *The Star*, 30 Sept. 2017, www.thestar.com/news/
  insight/2017/09/30/how-pk-subbans-dad-prepared-him-for-the-
  game-of-life.html.

Cotsonika, Nicholas J. "The Bulls Brothers: Subban Sibling
  Rivalry Makes NHL Debut." *Belleville Intelligencer*, 12 Dec.
  2017, www.intelligencer.ca/2017/12/12/the-bulls-brothers-
  subban-sibling-rivalry-makes-nhl-debut/wcm/a939490b-bff5-
  2df4-6e24-14362ac8c4ab.

"Karl Subban Is Canada's Ultimate Hockey Dad with
  Three Sons in NHL." *Canadian Immigrant*, 5 Jan. 2015,
  canadianimmigrant.ca/people/karl-subban-is-canadas-ultimate-
  hockey-dad-with-three-sons-in-nhl.

McGrath, Ben. "The Ice Breaker: Can P.K. Subban Win Over Hockey's Stoic Traditionalists?" *Huffington Post*, 15 Dec. 2014, www.huffingtonpost.com/2014/12/09/pk-subban_n_6295766.html.

"P.K. Subban, Hockey's Undisputed Most Stylish Man, Talks Suiting." *Sharp Magazine*, 27 Mar. 2018, sharpmagazine.com/2018/03/27/p-k-subban-hockeys-most-stylish-man-talks-suiting/.

Rexrode, Joe. "P.K. Subban's Latest Target – the Barrier between Police, Kids." *Tennessean*, 18 Dec. 2017, www.tennessean.com/story/sports/columnist/joe-rexrode/2017/12/19/p-k-subbans-latest-target-barrier-between-police-kids-nashville-predators-blue-line-buddies/963307001/.

Stubbs, Dave. "Subban Trade Leaves Montreal Stunned." *NHL*, 29 June 2016, www.nhl.com/news/subban-trade-leaves-montreal-stunned/c-281086100.

Vingan, Adam. "Rivalry Between P.K. Subban, Sidney Crosby Escalating during Stanley Cup Final." *Tennessean*, 9 June 2017, www.tennessean.com/story/sports/nhl/predators/2017/06/09/p-k-subban-sidney-crosby-rivalry-escalating-during-stanley-cup-final/383367001/.

INDEX

ABOUT THE AUTHOR

Teresa M. Walker has been a journalist for more than 30 years in Tennessee. Based in Nashville, she covers the NFL's Titans, the NHL's Predators, the NBA's Grizzlies, and a handful of college teams. She has covered a Stanley Cup Final, three Super Bowls, and five Olympics—including in 2018, when the US women's hockey team won a gold medal in South Korea.